who is God?

15 encounters with the Irreducible

Ryan McCoskey

Contents

Introduction

If you've ever read the book of Acts in the Bible, then you know that Paul spent quite a bit of time in prison. He agitated all kinds of people. Religious individuals like the Jews were offended by Paul because he insisted that God didn't accept people based on their moral performance or religious involvement.

Less-religious people like many of the Gentiles were also offended by Paul. He argued that no person could find a truly satisfying identity or a life of real meaning apart from faith in Jesus. At one point, he even threatened the economic stability of an entire region by encouraging people to become Christians and to stop purchasing idols of the Greek goddess Artemis.

Paul's teachings on Christianity didn't fit neatly into any category. The Gospel message caused friction in religious and irreligious communities alike.

The book of Acts tells us about a Roman governor named Felix who was *intrigued* by Paul. Felix didn't quite understand Christianity, and he was curious to find out why Paul's message was causing so much social upheaval. Felix visited Paul while he was in prison, and he asked Paul to explain Christianity to him.

"After some days Felix came with his wife Drusilla, who was Jewish, and he sent for Paul and heard him speak about faith in Christ Jesus. And as he reasoned about righteousness and self-control and the coming judgment, Felix was alarmed and said, 'Go away for the

present. When I get an opportunity I will summon you'" (Acts 24:24-25).

This interaction between Paul and Felix gives us three key pieces of information. First, we don't have a full account of Paul's talk with Felix, but we are told that Paul presented three concepts: *righteousness, self-control,* and *the coming judgment.*

This isn't too surprising because it aligns with much of what Jesus taught. Jesus clearly proclaimed that all people need to become righteous. He preached about sin and the great need we have for God's forgiveness. Jesus also said a lot about self-control. In one of his most well-known sayings Jesus tells us we cannot follow him unless we put to death the passions of our flesh (pick up our cross and deny ourselves).

Jesus warned people about the coming judgment, as well. He called for repentance: turning away from sin and living in obedience to God. All throughout the four gospels, Jesus teaches about God's justice and the reality of hell. So it isn't surprising that Paul covered these topics with Felix. He was simply restating much of what Jesus said.

We can't know exactly how that conversation unfolded, but we can imagine Paul saying this: *"God is going to judge all people because he is a just judge. All sin will be punished. But there is a way to avoid this punishment. You can become righteous by faith in Jesus and learn how to have self-control by setting your mind on God, rather than being enslaved to the passions of your body."*

It's not hard to imagine Paul saying this to Felix because he wrote this way. All throughout the New Testament, Paul talks about God's justice, our sin, righteousness through faith in Jesus, setting our minds on God, and overcoming our sinful urges, longings, and desires.

So the first thing to notice about Paul's conversation with Felix is what he said. Paul repeated much of what Jesus said. He told Felix that God was going to judge all people, and therefore, he needed to become righteous by faith in Jesus and learn self-control.

Secondly, we are told how Felix *emotionally* responded to Paul's words. He was alarmed. The word 'alarmed' is translated from the Greek word *emphobos*. It means to feel fear or to be greatly frightened. Though Paul was a helpless man in prison, unable to threaten Felix in any way, his description of Christianity provoked terror in Felix's heart. *Why?*

The only reasonable explanation is that Paul showed Felix some characteristics of God he had *never considered*. The concept of God's justice shook Felix. The idea that he needed to become righteous to avoid eternal punishment struck him. The teachings of Jesus on self-control shocked him.

Thirdly, we are told how Felix treated Paul. He told Paul to go away, essentially saying, *"Don't talk to me about this again. If I summon you, then you can talk to me. Otherwise, don't take it upon yourself to explain Christianity to me anymore."*

There are many people – even many Christians – who are like Felix. They don't quite understand Christianity. They have *some* grasp of it, and what they do believe about God is easy for them to believe. They may readily accept, for example, that God is loving and forgiving and merciful.

But their view of God is a *reduction*: they have reduced God by highlighting some of his characteristics and then muting, or *altogether ignoring*, other ones. The god they are imagining is a reduction of who God really is.

This book has been written to help you encounter the *irreducible* nature of the Christian God. He is a God of radical forgiveness and boundless compassion, but he's also a God of cosmic authority and righteous anger. When some of God's characteristics are highlighted and others are muted, a reduction is formed – a simplistic, man-made version.

A person cannot encounter the real God and not be shaken like Felix. The reality of God is overwhelming. But if we want to know God, then we must lay down our comfortable, man-made reduction and turn to the Bible to discover the fullness of his character.

If you're not a Christian, I still think this book could be of use to you. It will help you understand more about who the Christian God claims to be. Can you honestly say you *really* understand Christianity? Is there a chance you don't fully know what the Bible says about who God is?

If you are a Christian, my guess is you will respond to this book in one of two ways. You will either grow in your understanding and appreciation of who God is, or you will decide that what the Bible says about God is unreliable. If you opt for the latter, I encourage you to reflect on why you believe you're a Christian.

The truth is, there's no gain to be had by living in denial. If you find that you reject the Christian God, at least you can honestly assess your objections. Christians have always believed the Bible to be God's self-revelation: his communication to us of who he is. If you're not ready to accept the Christian God unless you can decide which of his characteristics suit you best, then it's likely you're not a Christian. It certainly doesn't have to stay that way.

Sometimes when we're bothered by a dear friend, we may wish they were different – that they were a little more of this, or a little less of that. But no such person exists. They're a figment of our imagination. When it comes to our friends, they *do* have some characteristics that are flawed, just like we do. But in God's character, there is no brokenness. He is who he is, and he's eternally righteous. You can trust him or reject him, but you can't change him.

You can decide to trust God and be a Christian. You can decide to reject the Christian God and not be a Christian. But there's no sense in reducing God to something that suits you and then claiming to be a Christian. The reduction you've made cannot possibly be real: it's just a set of characteristics you've arbitrarily assembled in your mind. A god like that can't know you or love you, and it certainly has no power to change you.

Day 1
More than Ordinary

Well, you've started day 1, which means you just committed yourself to 15 days with me. I'm being serious. You have been initiated. No turning back. Your 15-day journey has begun.

Let's be clear: I didn't write this book to merely intrigue you. I'm not interested in helping you think about airy platitudes. I'm in this to change you – to *radically* change you.

I've got a problem, though. It's a big problem too. I *can't* change you because I'm just like you. I'm just a guy who wrote a book you happen to be reading. I have no power to radically change your life – but God *does*. I seriously believe that.

A lot of what is called 'Christianity' today seems so impotent to change people who call themselves Christians. I've got a theory about it, and it's pretty simple: *Many Christians have reduced the God they claim to serve, and so the god they imagine makes no real difference in their life.*

Are you a Christian? You don't have to be to read this book. In fact, if you're not a Christian, I'm really glad you're here. I hope you get something valuable from this book. Truth be told, you may get *more* out of it than some Christians.

How can I say that? I can say it because it's a story that plays out again and again in the Bible. There are always people identifying with God who don't really know him. Starting with Cain in Genesis all the way through the New Testament, there are always people who have the *appearance* of godliness, and yet they deny God's power. The same story carries on still today.

If you're a Christian, you might feel picked on right now. Perhaps you're thinking, "Come on, man! I'm not the Apostle Paul! I'm just an ordinary person." Precisely. You *are* just an ordinary person. But that's not the problem. The problem is you're living like you've been created by an *ordinary god.* Your expectations are low because your view of God is faulty.

Over these 15 days, I'd like to introduce you to a God who's worth trusting. I'm not using vague, religious language. I literally mean that you can trust God – the real God – with every part of your life. If you're not a Christian, I want you to become one, *but only if God really meets you.* Give this book a chance. If nothing else, you'll gain a better understanding of who the Christian God claims to be.

These 15 days are all about encountering God. Here's what this means for you:

1.) *Commit to spending 15 days with me in this book right now.*

This is not a self-help book. This isn't a diet plan, or a workout routine, or a '10 steps to success' handbook. I want to help you meet with God, but don't think of this book like a ladder you can climb. Think of it like a window on a ceiling you can't reach, but can see through. Meeting God is not about your efforts – it's about your openness. This isn't about you making something happen, it's about you meeting Someone who can't be reached by mere human exertion.

I'm asking you to commit – to honestly, seriously commit – because we don't just choose to encounter God. *God meets us.* You're opening yourself up to hear what God might say to you. You're not calling the shots. You're the patient, and he's the doctor. It's your place to sit in the waiting room until he calls your name. You don't need to do anything right now; you just need to listen.

This isn't a process we get to shortcut. Either dive in headfirst, or shelf this book. If I sound callous, please know my words are coming from a place of love. I don't want you to waste this opportunity.

2.) *Read this each day for 15 days.*

This book, in and of itself, is powerless to change you. It may intrigue you, or entertain you, or teach you, but it won't radically change you. That's God's domain. Unlike the words in this book, the words of Scripture are *alive*. No, I'm not talking about organic life, I'm talking about *spiritual life*. The Bible can radically change you because God speaks into your life through the Scriptures.

Think of it this way: As I'm writing this sentence, it's being logged into history. It's now in the past. It's locked away, sitting lifeless in the annals of time. Likewise, when you read the Bible you're reading something that was written in the past by an author to a particular audience.

But there's a major difference. When you read the Bible, God brings the meaning of His Word to life in your heart and speaks directly to you. I'm not talking about some hocus pocus experience. I'm saying that when you apply your heart and mind to what the Bible says, God applies it to *you* – he cuts into you. *He reads you.* He shows you what's in your heart and exposes your motives, desires, and intentions.

This is why I'll direct you to read the Bible verses I've provided for each day. I can teach you something, but I can't climb into your heart and reach the deep places. *God can.*

> Each day the Bible verses will be provided in a sidebar just like this one.

3.) *Every day will end with a prayer, and I encourage you to take it seriously.*

Prayer is an act of humility and boldness. We are humbly acknowledging that our efforts aren't enough, and we're boldly believing that God is powerful to act. Let's talk about how Jesus prayed. He prayed like this: Your kingdom come. Your will be done.

Give us our daily bread. Forgive us our sin. Lead us not into temptation. Deliver us from evil.

How does God's kingdom come? *He sends it.* How is God's will done? *He wills it.* How do we receive our daily provision? *He gives it.* How do we deal with our sin? *He forgives it.* How do we withstand temptation? *He leads us away from it.* How do we escape evil? *He delivers us.*

The act of prayer, in its very essence, is a confession of *need.* When we pray, we are admitting we need help, and we are submitting to the One who can help us. The prayer I've provided for each day is a very important part of your encounter with God. Don't rush through it. Be intentional. If you're not a Christian, it will likely make you feel awkward. I encourage you to work through it anyway.

4.) *Do not read ahead, and throughout each day, reflect on what you learned about God.*

This journey is toward transformation, not education. The goal is not to simply fill your mind. This book won't make you an accomplished theologian. But it will give you an opportunity to encounter a God who can radically change you – eternally – for the better.

After reading each day, consider what you learned. Think on it. Let it trickle from your mind down into your heart. Just take it day by day.

That's enough for now. Let's pray together.

———————————— ◆ ————————————

God,

I don't like to feel needy or dependent. I want to feel in control of my life. I want to believe that I can change myself, but you claim that only you can truly change me. I've committed to meet with you for 15 days, and so I ask you to meet with me.

Speak to me through the Bible and this book. Read my heart. Go into the deep places in my soul. Draw out the intentions and motivations of my heart.

Be gentle with me. Treat me according to your steadfast love and your abounding grace. Walk with me. Fill me with joy and peace as I genuinely seek you.

Amen.

Day 2
Taking Ownership

Read Joshua 23:6-8, 11.

"Therefore, be very strong to keep and to do all that is written in the Book of the Law of Moses, turning aside from it neither to the right hand nor to the left, that you may not mix with these nations remaining among you or make mention of the names of their gods or swear by them or serve them or bow down to them, but you shall cling to the Lord your God just as you have done to this day. Be very careful, therefore, to love the Lord your God."

Joshua became Israel's chief leader after Moses died, and at this point in Israel's history, Joshua was old and near his death. So he gathered all the leaders of Israel and spoke to them.

He encouraged them to be strong. How did he define strength? *Keep and do all that is written in the Book of the Law.* Joshua warned them about 'mixing' with the nations that surrounded them. Why was Joshua so concerned? He feared they would be allured by false gods and would begin to *swear by them or serve them or bow down to them.*

Joshua used some pretty forceful words. Read Joshua 24:14.

Notice the second half of the verse: *Put away the gods that your fathers served...* Perhaps Joshua's concern makes more sense to you now. Joshua forcefully warned Israel's leaders because *he knew what kind of example had been set for them*, and it wasn't a very good one.

> "Now therefore fear the Lord and serve him in sincerity and in faithfulness. Put away the gods that your fathers served beyond the River and in Egypt, and serve the Lord."

Here's essentially what Joshua was saying: *'I love you, and I want what's best for you, so please listen to me – I've seen the consequences of wandering from God. I saw how it destroyed your parents. I know you were not given a great example to follow, and that breaks my heart for you. But don't make that your excuse. Take ownership of your relationship with God. Seek Him. Be very careful to love Him because if you adopt & worship false gods like your parents did, it will not go well for you.'*

All of us have been influenced by others. Some people have invested in you, and it's changed your life for the better. Some people have harmed you, and you still carry the scars – emotional, physical, or both. Some of you grew up surrounded by great examples to follow, but many of you grew up in painful brokenness. That genuinely breaks my heart for you.

Listen closely to these words and know they are spoken in love: Your character flaws, your harmful habits, and your sinful cravings can likely be *explained* by your past, *but that doesn't excuse them.*

You're not a passive machine that can only do what you've been shown. You're not like a cup – you don't have to pour out what's been put into you. Perhaps the idea of God puts a bad taste in your mouth because your parents are very moralistic people who practice their religion but show little sign of genuine love. That certainly helps to explain why someone might reject God, but it's only an explanation. It's not an excuse.

Maybe your dad is an angry man. That could explain some things about you, but it doesn't excuse your anger. Perhaps your older brother, who you really looked up to, introduced you to alcohol. That could explain some things about you, but it doesn't excuse your addiction. It's possible that you grew up poor and worked incredibly hard for everything you now have. That could explain some things about you, but it doesn't excuse your greed.

We have to take ownership. We have to own our flaws. Own our sin. Own our decisions.

Right now you may be wondering, 'What about God's love? What about forgiveness?' You need to understand that this is love. Love does not always comfort. God's love doesn't aim at always making us feel cheery about ourselves. God's love aims at making us whole. This is part of the process.

As for forgiveness – that word has no meaning apart from sin and wrongdoing. We first need to own our sin, then we can be forgiven. If we don't own it, then we're not taking responsibility. We're blameshifting.

Some of you may be thinking about someone other than yourself. You're thinking about your spouse who really needs to change, or that opinionated religious person at work, or those youthful rabble who don't respect authority and seem to have such weird political views. But they're not reading this book right now. You are.

If my words are bringing other people into your mind, and you're not reflecting on the ways you tend to justify your own sin, then I encourage you to own your self-righteousness. Maybe you easily fall into arrogance and imagine you're superior to others because you are genuinely more intelligent or more disciplined than many people you know. That helps to explain your arrogance, but it doesn't excuse it.

Pride will destroy you. If you fail to take ownership for your sin, it will eventually kill your soul. Read Isaiah 2:11-12.

God has a particular way of doing things. If we refuse to humble ourselves, then God will take care of that for us. *He has a day against all that is proud and lofty.* Surrender your pride. Own your shortcomings. Take a seat on the floor now, and a day will come when he puts you on a throne. Put yourself on a throne now, and a day will come when he casts you away from all that is good.

> "The haughty looks of man shall be brought low, and the lofty pride of men shall be humbled, and the Lord alone will be exalted in that day. For the Lord of hosts has a day against all that is proud and lofty, against all that is lifted up – and it shall be brought low."

It may be difficult for you to believe this, but *God loves you more than you can imagine.* His love, however, is not a license to destroy yourself and others. His love aims to make you whole, and proud people don't want to be made whole – they think they're doing just fine on their own. Don't take the bait. Instead, take ownership.

Let's pray together.

God,

When my flaws are exposed – when my sin is before me – I often try to pin the responsibility on someone else. When I do something impressive, I like to think about how my hard work and dedication made it happen. But when I do something foolish, I like to point out how others influenced me. I try to avoid taking ownership because I am prideful. Please forgive me.

I know you oppose proud people and lift up humble people. Teach me to be humble. Help me to lower myself. Forgive me for downplaying my own sin and highlighting the sin I see in other people. Teach me how to take ownership for my own sin. Rid me of my self-righteousness. Convict me of my excuses.

I know you love broken, sinful people. Thank you for loving me. Renovate my heart. Crush my pride and radically change me.

Amen.

Day 3

Hope for the Ungodly

Read Isaiah 55:8-9.

What does it mean to be ungodly? In simplest terms, it means to be unlike God. That's the main point of the passage you just read. You and I are ungodly because *we are not like God*.

"For my thoughts are not your thoughts, neither are your ways my ways, declares the Lord. For as the heavens are higher than the earth, so are my ways higher than your ways and my thoughts than your thoughts."

You live in two spheres – an inner world and an outer world. Your inner world is made up of your thoughts, emotions, aspirations, and motives. Your outer world is made up of your actions and words. You are unlike God in both spheres. *His thoughts are not your thoughts, neither are his ways your ways.*

Even more, the degree of difference between you and God is *colossal*. God is not just a little better, or stronger, or wiser than you – he is utterly different from you, so much so that you are 'ungodly' compared to him. You are nothing like him. *As the heavens are higher than earth, his ways and thoughts are higher than yours.*

This poses a serious problem for us: God has called us to a high standard – a standard he *requires* us to keep. Christians often call this standard his law. It's important to recognize that God's law is not just a list of things to do, or not to do. Rather, his law is an extension of his character.

This means we cannot keep God's law unless we share his character. That's a problem. We are ungodly people who don't share God's character, but we will be held accountable to his law.

This is the fundamental and most serious problem that every person faces. We must come to grips with it. Even though something deep within us tells us our words and actions matter – that we *are* called to a high standard – we try to suppress this intuition.

Read Psalm 10:13.

> "Why does the wicked renounce God and say in his heart, 'You will not call to account?'"

We want to believe that God won't call us to account because we know we haven't lived up to his standard. Something in us is always evaluating and judging how we're living our lives. We carry with us an oppressive sense of right and wrong, and we can't seem to get rid of it.

This is because we are under God's law. He has implanted a sense of it into our hearts, and one day he will call us to account for how we chose to live our lives.

Read Romans 3:19.

> "Now we know that whatever the law says it speaks to those who are under the law, so that every mouth may be stopped, and the whole world may be held accountable to God."

What can we do? How do we fix this problem?

First, the bad news: *You can't fix this problem.* This isn't something you can solve by trying harder. No amount of learning, training, or experience can make any difference at all.

You are in-over-your-head to a cosmic level. You are an ungodly person, called to a godly standard.

What you need is a *rescue*.

Now, the good news: Read Romans 5:6.

God has somehow overcome the yawning chasm between us and him, and it involves a Christ – or a Savior – dying for us: *the ungodly.* What kind of a God dies for the ungodly? The God of the Christians

> "For while we were still weak, at the right time Christ died for the ungodly."

dies for the ungodly. Tomorrow we'll begin unpacking the nature of this God.

Let's pray together.

———————————————◆———————————————

God,

I'm thankful that your ways are higher than mine. Thank you for being more forgiving than I can imagine, and more powerful than I can understand.

I am an ungodly person. I'm nothing like you. In the depth of my heart, I know my words and actions matter, but I don't like thinking about it because I know I haven't lived up to your standard. I am under your law, and I've failed to keep it.

I am a weak and ungodly person, but the Bible says you died for weak and ungodly people. Help me understand that. Help me believe that. Show me more about who you are and teach me how to live a life that honors you and others.

Amen.

Day 4

Unique Oneness

Read Mark 13:31-32.

> "Heaven and earth will pass away, but my words will not pass away. But concerning that day or that hour, no one knows, not even the angels in heaven, nor the Son, but only the Father."

Several times in the Bible, Jesus claims to be God. He exercises an authority that only God could have, and he says things about himself that only God could say. Jesus cannot be just a good moral teacher because a good teacher wouldn't lie about being God. We can either take Jesus at his word, or we must assume he is a liar.

Jesus, without reservation, called himself God, but he also talked about his 'Father' all throughout the four gospels. According to Jesus, there are some things that only the Father knows, like when the world will end. Nobody knows when this will happen – no person, no angel, not even Jesus – just the Father.

The Bible introduces us to a God of great complexity. It says he is a single God and also the *only* God. He's not one of many gods in a pantheon.

Read Deuteronomy 6:4-5.

God is one, not many. We're called to love him and him alone with all our heart, soul, and might.

> "Hear, O Israel: The Lord our God, the Lord is one. You shall love the Lord your God with all your heart and with all your soul and with all your might."

But there is something very unique about God's oneness. Within him there are *three distinct persons*: the Father, the Son, and the Spirit. This is called the 'Trinity.' God is a community within himself. There is diversity in God, but no division. There is unity in God, but no uniformity. He is one, and within that oneness there are three divine persons. He is perfectly united and perfectly diverse.

Some have argued that this is far too complex. They say if God was real he would be simpler to understand. But that makes no sense at all. Science has taught us that everything we see is very complex. All material things are made of molecules, which are formed by atoms – rich layers of complex structures that go far beyond any simple explanation.

If God really exists, and if he created everything we see, then isn't it reasonable to assume that he is *more* complex than the things he's made? What is more complex: a sculpture or the artist who sculpts it? The artist is *always* more complex than his or her art. Why should it be any different with God?

Jesus speaks not only of his Father, but also of the Spirit. Read John 15:26.

The Spirit, also called the Helper, comes from the Father like Jesus. But the Spirit is not the same person as Jesus. In the verse you just read, you can observe all three persons of the Trinity: *Jesus* talking about the *Spirit* who comes from the *Father*.

> "But when the Helper comes, whom I will send to you from the Father, the Spirit of truth, who proceeds from the Father, he will bear witness about me."

You may be wondering why God's unique oneness matters. Understanding that God is a Trinity is important because without it the Gospel is senseless, and the Gospel is our only hope. We cannot be forgiven and redeemed by God apart from the Gospel, and the Gospel is rooted in the Bible's description of who God is: three distinct persons, yet only one God.

God's unique oneness is also important for understanding our desire to know others and to be known by others. God is a community within himself, and according to the Bible, God made us *in his image*. We don't share God's divine nature, but our longing to be in fulfilling relationships with other people is something we feel because of God's imprint upon us. He made us that way.

When Jesus was asked about marriage, for example, he directly connected God's image to marriage. Just as God is three distinct persons and yet only one God, a man and a woman – who are *also* distinctly different in their complementary gender structure – come together in marriage and become 'one flesh.'

Marriage is a God-ordained symbol that speaks to his nature. In any piece of art, if you look close enough, you can discover the identity of the artist. When we look at how God created us and how he designed us to relate to one another, we can see traces of his nature.

God is the best example of perfect unity, and God is also the best example of perfect diversity. Within God there is beautiful diversity and perfect unity. Three, and yet only one. We can understand God's nature better by considering each person of the Trinity, which is what we'll do over the next three days.

Let's pray together.

———————————————— ◈ ————————————————

God,

I can't fully understand what it means that you are one God, and yet three divine persons. I think of you in much simpler ways. In fact, I often see the world around me as much more complex than you.

But you claim to be the Creator of all that surrounds me. You're the artist. You are more complex than all you have made. I don't appreciate the mystery of your nature often enough.

Thank you for creating me in your image and giving me a hunger for satisfying relationships. Thank you for the beauty of your unity and your diversity. Open my eyes to better understand you as I think on your nature over the next three days.

Amen.

Day 5

The All-Knowing Father

Read Matthew 6:7-8.

The Bible doesn't portray the Father as a distant character who is out of touch with us. *The Father knows what you need before you ask him.* The Father is all-knowing. He is the grand designer of all things. The powerful creator. The invisible God who has never been seen.

> "And when you pray, do not heap up empty phrases as the Gentiles do, for they think that they will be heard for their many words. Do not be like them, for your Father knows what you need before you ask him."

The Father is sovereign: he is the supreme ruler, limitless in his authority, able to bring all his plans to pass, boundless, unstoppable.

Read Proverbs 19:21.

> "Many are the plans in the mind of a man, but it is the purpose of the Lord that will stand."

The Father is not held captive by our plans, ideas, or purposes. We make our plans, and we have our ideas about how things ought to be, but *it is the purpose of the Lord that will stand*. His plans will come to pass. His ideas about how things ought to be are supreme. His purposes for us will stand.

The Father shows us the *transcendence* of God. He transcends our world. He is more expansive than the universe. He is beyond the stars. He surpasses all human comprehension. He is not a force that can be found in nature – he is not constricted within the world we see around us. He is the creator of it all, outside of it, completely independent of it.

When the Apostle Paul was in Athens he shared about the Father with many people, and he highlighted God's transcendence and independence.

Read Acts 17:24-27.

It's common for us to invert our relationship with God: instead of recognizing that he is independent from us, we see ourselves as independent from him. But we aren't independent from God. *He gives life and breath to all mankind.*

God is not served by human hands. He doesn't *need* anything. God is not dependent upon us for his well-being. God demands our worship, but it's not because he needs it – on the contrary, *we* need it. As we worship God, we are recognizing that he is the all-knowing Father who sustains our life.

"The God who made the world and everything in it, being Lord of heaven and earth, does not live in temples made by man, nor is he served by human hands, as though he needed anything, since he himself gives to all mankind life and breath and everything. And he made from one man every nation of mankind to live on all the face of the earth, having determined allotted periods and the boundaries of their dwelling place, that they should seek God, in the hope that they might feel their way toward him and find him. Yet he is actually not far from each one of us."

God's sovereign power is breathtaking. He created the first man and woman, and from them he made all the various nations of mankind.

Even more, he decides how long nations will flourish and how far their boundaries will reach. *He determines their allotted periods and the boundaries of their dwelling place.*

The Father makes us feel small – and rightly so. His infinite power puts our finite lives into perspective. His unlimited control stands in stark contrast to our lack of control. His exhaustive knowledge of all things overwhelms our limited understanding. The Father humbles us.

Although God is transcendent, existing outside of the seen world, he is also *immanent*. He is near. God is beyond the stars, and yet you can approach him as you read this book. *He is actually not far from each one of us.*

The Father is righteous, and we are not. He is pure light, and we are creatures of shadow. He deals in nothing but truth, and we are skilled in half-truths and sometimes complete lies. We cannot approach the Father in our sin. In the Old Testament book of Deuteronomy, God calls himself a *consuming fire.* As the light eradicates all darkness, his presence drives out all who indulge in sin. That's certainly a problem because *we are sinners.*

But there is hope for us. There is hope for the ungodly. We can find redemption and be at peace with the Father *through his Son.* We will think on him tomorrow.

Let's pray together.

———————————— ◈ ————————————

Father God,

You claim to know what I need more than I know what I need. I make plans for my life, and I have ideas about how it should go, but it is your plans that will stand. Teach me to spend less time fixating on my plans. Make me receptive to your plans.

I tend to put you in a box. I restrict you in my mind. I make you small enough to fit in my pocket, but you're bigger than the universe.

Thank you for being near and far – beyond my imagination, and yet close at hand. Remind me that you don't need anything and that you're not dependent upon me. Remind me that I am utterly dependent upon you.

Amen.

Day 6

The Son of God

Read Hebrews 1:1-3.

"Long ago, at many times and in many ways, God spoke to our fathers by the prophets, but in these last days he has spoken to us by his Son, whom he appointed the heir of all things, through whom also he created the world. He is the radiance of the glory of God and the exact imprint of his nature, and he upholds the universe by the word of his power. After making purification for sins, he sat down at the right hand of the Majesty on high."

There was a time when God spoke to people through prophets – mere, mortal men and women. God would raise up a prophet for a time, but because of their natural limitations, a new prophet would have to come after. Death, sickness, or disobedience to God ended their tenure.

Jesus, the Son of God, is the *final* and *forever* prophet of God. Death and sickness have no power over him, and he is thoroughly perfect like his Father. Jesus is eternal. He is the heir of all things, and the Father created the universe through him. Jesus is so much like his Father that he is the *radiance of God's glory* and the *exact imprint of God's nature*.

At one point during his life, Jesus claimed that if anyone truly knew him, they also truly knew the Father. This powerfully illustrates the unique oneness that Jesus shares with Father God. When we read about Jesus in the Scriptures and get to know him, we are learning about the Father as well. We come to know the Father through the Son.

What's so amazing about Jesus is that in him the nature of God and the nature of man are eternally interwoven.

Read John 1:1-3, 14.

Something (or Someone) called the *Word* has existed for all time. The Word has always been with God, and the Word *is* God. When God created the universe, all things were made through the Word. So who or what is this Word? *The Word became flesh and dwelt among us.*

"In the beginning was the Word, and the Word was with God, and the Word was God. He was in the beginning with God. All things were made through him, and without him was not any thing made that was made. And the Word became flesh and dwelt among us, and we have seen his glory, glory as of the only Son from the Father, full of grace and truth."

Jesus is the Word.

Jesus existed before he was birthed into human history. He has existed for all eternity past with God the Father. But when he came as a man something new was born – God clothed in the flesh of man. Jesus is fully God and fully man. Before Jesus' coming, God had created man, but God didn't share the nature of man. But now, in Jesus, God's nature is interwoven with man's nature. *Jesus is the bridge between finite mankind and an infinite God.*

Christian theology makes such a big deal of Jesus' death on a cross because his death is what makes it possible for sinners to know God. It's the most *scandalous* event in all history. Jesus, who is fully God and perfectly sinless, was murdered by sinners who were cut off from God and enslaved to sin. Through Jesus' unjust death, God made a way for unjust sinners to *know* him.

Read Colossians 1:19-22.

> "For in him all the fullness of God was pleased to dwell, and through him to reconcile to himself all things, whether on earth or in heaven, making peace by the blood of his cross. And you, who once were alienated and hostile in mind, doing evil deeds, he has now reconciled in his body of flesh by his death, in order to present you holy and blameless and above reproach before him."

Jesus makes peace by the blood of his cross. He brings reconciliation. *How?* Jesus can make us holy, blameless, and above reproach before God by his *death*. Though we are alienated from God and hostile toward his work, we can be reconciled to him through Jesus. *You, who once were alienated and hostile in mind, doing evil deeds, he has now reconciled in his body of flesh by his death.*

Because Jesus is fully man, he is our *representative*. Jesus stood in for all mankind on the cross. He died to satisfy the Father's righteous anger against our sin. Jesus is our substitute.

But because Jesus is also fully God, he is our *savior* too. His death is powerful to save us because he was innocent. He was sinless, spotless, and perfect. Jesus' nature of complete man and complete God gives him the distinct ability to redeem us by his death. He is our representative and our rescuer – our substitute and our savior. Jesus, and Jesus alone, is capable of fulfilling these two roles.

The good news of the Gospel is not only that Jesus died for our sin, but also that God *resurrected* him from the dead. Why did God raise Jesus from the dead? Because his death was a *perfect sacrifice*. Death is a curse of sin. We die because we are sinners. Jesus never sinned – he was the spotless Son of God. He didn't die as a result of his sin, but as a sacrifice to make atonement for *our* sin.

When God raised Jesus from the dead, he was proclaiming the good news that Jesus really did make a perfect atonement for our sin. Everything that separated us from God was cast upon Jesus, and he died to take our punishment away *forever*. Jesus *became* the curse of sin for us, and through his death and resurrection, he broke the curse.

The Bible teaches that Jesus' life, death, and resurrection is still supremely meaningful for us today, even though he was born more than 2,000 years ago. How can an ancient historical event impact our lives deeply today? That's where the Spirit comes in.

Let's pray together.

Jesus,

The Bible says you were with the Father from the beginning. The Father created all things through you. You are divine, and yet you chose to be born in human flesh. Even more, you willingly died a criminal's death to take my punishment away and to reconcile me to the Father.

You have a heart for those who are separated from the Father. You love those who are hostile to the work of God in their lives. You love them so much you died for them. You represented mankind on the cross, and you rescue us from eternal death. You died an unjust death to redeem unjust sinners like me.

Thank you for loving me apart from my moral performance. Thank you for making peace by the blood of your cross, and making it possible for me to have a relationship with the Father. Thank you for choosing to leave your glory in heaven, and instead taking on the humble frame of a man for me.

Teach me how to love the Father like you, and teach me how to love others like you.

Amen.

Day 7

The Spirit of Truth

Read John 14:25-26.

"These things I have spoken to you while I am still with you. But the Helper, the Holy Spirit, whom the Father will send in my name, he will teach you all things and bring to your remembrance all that I have said to you."

Jesus cared about the spiritual maturity of his disciples. He wanted them to be followers and leaders: followers of God and leaders of people. Jesus was not content with teaching them just once, giving them something to think about, and then moving on. Jesus was interested in a lifelong partnership with them, walking with each one of them every day.

Jesus could not do this in the flesh. He could only be in one place at one time. But the Holy Spirit *can* do this. When Jesus ascended to heaven after his resurrection, the Father sent the Holy Spirit – the Helper – to walk with us every hour of every day. *He teaches us all things and brings to remembrance all that Jesus taught.*

The Holy Spirit is the one who applies the finished work of Jesus to us. He helps us sense God's love in our hearts. He brings conviction in our lives when we're living in sin, and he compels us to walk in a manner worthy of our calling. The Holy Spirit interacts with us as we read the Bible and pray. He guides us into truth and gives us strength to withstand temptation.

The Spirit is one with the Father and the Son. The Father is the architect, the grand designer, the chief authority who sends both the Son and the Spirit. Jesus, the Son, is the exact imprint of God's nature who came to secure our redemption through his death and resurrection. Jesus is the one who came to us, took on human flesh, and became our representative and rescuer.

The Spirit, then, is the one who daily resides with every redeemed Christian. He keeps us connected with the love of the Father and the teaching of the Son. He attends every worship gathering with us, he comforts us in our mourning, he rejoices with us as we celebrate, he gives us wisdom to speak into the lives of others, and he does the heavy lifting of transforming us into people who live and love like Jesus.

Read Romans 8:13-15.

The Spirit of God works in us, which means he causes our lives to *practically change*. The Holy Spirit gives us power to put our sinful deeds to death. He leads us. He doesn't just change how we think. His influence upon us is not theoretical – it's practical. He affects our real, everyday lives.

"For if you live according to the flesh you will die, but if by the Spirit you put to death the deeds of the body, you will live. For all who are led by the Spirit of God are sons of God. For you did not receive the spirit of slavery to fall back into fear, but you have received the Spirit of adoption as sons, by whom we cry, 'Abba! Father!'"

Without the Spirit of God, Christianity would just be a philosophy, a way of thinking. It would have no power to actually change us. But because the Father gives us the Holy Spirit, we can have *real* newness of life.

One of the greatest ministries of the Spirit is his work to constantly remind us that we are free from judgment because of our faith in Jesus. *We did not receive a spirit of slavery that causes us to live in fear*. We don't have to fear that God will abandon us because of our sin. We don't have to worry that he will revoke the work of Jesus from our hearts. If we are in Christ, we are sons and daughters of God and free from all punishment.

The Holy Spirit helps us wrestle with the reality of our adoption. He stimulates spiritual growth in us not by threatening us with punishment, but by reminding us that through our faith in Jesus, we are beloved sons and daughters of God who no longer need to live in fear.

We change because of the Spirit. He is the catalyst for all the spiritual growth in our lives. We cannot know the Father, except by knowing the Son. And we cannot walk with Jesus and know his heart without the Spirit of God. The Gospel is good news. *We are free in Christ*. But the Gospel is powerless without the Triune nature of God. The Father, the Son, and the Holy Spirit all play a crucial role in our redemption.

Let's pray together.

Holy Spirit,

I am so very capable of reducing real Christian faith to an impotent system of thinking. I can be hostile to your work in my life. Sometimes I deceive myself and believe that my beliefs prove I have spiritual maturity, even though my life may not evidence much real change.

Apply the work of Christ to my heart. Pour a powerful sense of God's love into me. Help me walk in real newness of life, to fight against my sinful passions, and to experience genuine growth.

Thank you for convicting me of my sin so I can walk in a manner worthy of my calling. Thank you for bringing to remembrance in my heart and mind the teachings of Jesus. Compel me to meet you daily in the Bible and in prayer.

Amen.

Day 8

Contra-conditional Love

Read Luke 13:2-5.

It's rather common to hear people describing God's love as unconditional. In one sense, this is accurate. God has created every person. He has imprinted his image into every human being. This makes all people precious in God's sight. In this sense, God's love is unconditional. We don't have to meet any conditions to receive it. He simply loves us!

"Do you think that these Galileans were worse sinners than all the other Galileans, because they suffered in this way? No, I tell you; but unless you repent, you will all likewise perish. Or those eighteen on whom the tower in Siloam fell and killed them: do you think that they were worse offenders than all the others who lived in Jerusalem? No, I tell you; but unless you repent, you will all likewise perish."

But in another sense, this is not a helpful description of God's love. Because we are created in God's image, he does love us – but that doesn't mean he's going to *redeem* every person. God's redeeming love is *not* unconditional. We must meet a condition in order to receive God's redeeming love. *We must repent.*

Repentance is an intentional, heartfelt decision to turn away from our sin, and it includes admitting we are deeply flawed people who need God's forgiveness, wisdom, and grace. Repentance is not just for *some* people. God calls all of us to repent of our sin, to turn away from trusting in ourselves, and to trust Jesus.

It's easy to think that some people need to repent of their sin far more than others need to. Generally speaking, we tend to see sin as a large issue in other people's lives, and a small issue in our own. When other people suffer (especially people who bother us) it's common for us to think, *'they probably brought that upon themselves.'* When *we* suffer, it's common for us to think, *'why is this happening to me? I don't deserve this!'*

The idea of karma suggests that disastrous events happen to people who have done something to deserve punishment, and likewise, that good things happen to people who have proved themselves worthy in some way.

Jesus directly refuted this kind of thinking. *Do you think that some people are worse sinners than others because they died in some extraordinary way? No, they are not. If you don't repent, you will perish with them.*

Apparently a tower had fallen on some people in Jerusalem, and many assumed this was God's special judgment upon those who died. Some figured that the people who were crushed by the tower must have been particularly bad. Jesus taught otherwise. He said that all who refuse to repent will perish.

Repentance is a requirement. God's redeeming love is *conditional*: We must repent of our sin and turn to Jesus. This is a condition we must meet. All who fail to meet it will not receive God's forgiveness and grace.

Rather than describing God's redeeming love as unconditional, it would be more helpful to describe it as *contra-conditional*. There is a condition we must meet, but it's *contrary* to what we think. We would think that a God of such perfection and holiness would require us to prove ourselves worthy of him. We expect the condition to be something like, 'keep all of God's laws and memorize the Bible, and then you can be redeemed.'

But that's not the condition. Thank God that's not the condition! The condition is simply this: *Recognize that you could never prove yourself good enough, stop trusting in yourself and your own wisdom, and start trusting God and his wisdom.* God's redeeming love is contra-conditional in the sense that the condition is contrary to what we would expect. We assume he will demand us to perfectly keep his law. Instead, he demands that we humble ourselves, submit to God's wisdom, and trust Jesus.

Read Romans 2:4.

God is so kind to us. He could punish us for all our sin right now, but he doesn't. God is astoundingly patient with us. He could give up on us right now, but he won't. God is slow to anger. He could bury us under his wrath, but instead he withholds it from us. God freely gives us the riches of his kindness, patience, and forbearance.

> "Or do you presume on the riches of his kindness and forbearance and patience, not knowing that God's kindness is meant to lead you to repentance?"

However, these qualities of God are meant to produce something valuable in your life. God intends that they would lead you to *repentance.* Every person who refuses to recognize their sin and trust Jesus will see an *end* to God's kindness, patience, and forbearance. These gifts from God are not to be presumed upon. We shouldn't take them for granted.

At face value, this can feel an awful lot like cosmic manipulation. You might be asking yourself, '*So is God kind, patient, and slow to anger just to manipulate me into loving him?*' It's understandable why you might feel this way, but you're looking at it all wrong. You're not on equal ground with God. He's not your peer, he's your Creator. He is unstained by sin, and you're afflicted with it.

God isn't obligated to give us *any* kindness, patience, or forbearance. They are gifts of his grace. He gives us these gifts because he delights in our redemption. But if we make ourselves unredeemable creatures, then we will not be redeemed. If we harden our hearts to God and justify our sin, then we will not receive God's forgiveness or redeeming grace.

God loves you, but he isn't going to enable you to live in unrepentant sin. He isn't manipulating you – he is *inviting* you. God will warmly embrace you as the father embraced his prodigal son in the Luke 15 parable. If you refuse to come, you will not receive the redeeming embrace of the Father. Meet the condition. Repent. Trust Jesus and his wisdom for your life.

Let's pray together.

God,

It is so easy to presume on the riches of your kindness, patience, and forbearance. In fact, sometimes I feel entitled to them. When I face suffering, difficulty, or disappointment, I am tempted to be angry with you because I feel like you owe me something better. I don't see your patience with me as a gift often enough.

Show me the places in my life where I'm not trusting you. In what ways do I rationalize my sin? Am I refusing to repent of some sinful pattern in my life? Take me to task. Don't let me wander from you. I desperately need your redeeming grace, so please help me to repent.

Thank you for sending Jesus to fulfill all your laws on my behalf. Thank you for not requiring me to perfectly keep your law in order to receive your redeeming love. Fill me with gratitude for Jesus. Draw my heart to him. Teach me to trust him in everything.

Amen.

Day 9

Daily Discipline

Read Hebrews 12:7, 11.

The Bible refers to Christians as God's children – his sons and daughters. This should help us tremendously in our efforts to understand how God loves us. God feels a great sense of responsibility for us. Just as a father loves his children simply because they are his children, God loves us the same way.

"It is for discipline that you have to endure. God is treating you as sons. For what son is there whom his father does not discipline? For the moment all discipline seems painful rather than pleasant, but later it yields the peaceful fruit of righteousness to those who have been trained by it."

Good fathers love their children even when they fail, and God loves his children even when they sin. Children bear the name of their father, and Christians represent God. Good fathers encourage their children. They comfort them in distress and reassure them in the face of hardship. God does this for his children too.

But good fathers also *discipline* their children. A good father understands that his child, in his or her youth, inexperience, and ignorance, does not understand reality as it really is. Good fathers observe when their child acts foolishly, and they set out to root that foolishness out of them. Good fathers discipline in a spirit of love and honest concern.

Even the best human fathers sin. They discipline in anger at times, or they neglect their responsibility to lead and guide their children. But God never sins. He disciplines perfectly. He knows precisely what we need. He sees all the foolishness in our hearts, and he knows our every motive, our deepest desires, and our hidden intentions.

God loves us, and he understands the fullness of reality exactly as it is. Nothing is unclear to him. He doesn't wonder whether or not his actions are wise, or timely, or effective. He *is* wisdom. God knows what our future holds. He knows the characteristics we must have in order to face that future, and he is dedicated to preparing us.

Read Proverbs 3:11-12.

> "My son, do not despise the Lord's discipline or be weary of his reproof, for the Lord reproves him whom he loves, as a father the son in whom he delights."

Human parents are limited in their capacity. They discipline with verbal reprimands, or time-outs, or spankings. Good parents try to understand the motives of their child's heart; they work to address not only outward behavior, but also inward desires. But they are only human.

God, on the other hand, controls the universe. He is not limited in any way. So his discipline has a much wider scope. God sometimes brings financial struggle into a Christian's life to teach him or her that trusting in money is foolish. He sometimes allows stress to fill our lives to show us that nothing in this world can provide real, lasting comfort and satisfaction.

God's discipline is weaved into our daily lives. We learn hard lessons about ourselves, about others, and about the world, and it helps us see a little more of reality as it really is.

The goal of God's discipline is *always* our good. We will, at times, feel that God is being ruthlessly cold towards us. We can grow so weary of having a God who is constantly at work in us: molding, chiseling, challenging, changing, removing, instilling, re-making.

Although discipline is painful, we can rest in this hope: God disciplines his children because he *loves* his children. The Bible clearly teaches that every Christian is being prepared for the same destination. We will spend eternity in the holy presence of God. We are being readied for our reward. God's discipline in our lives is not in vain.

Sometimes a person will confess that they feel like God is punishing them. God does punish, but he *never* punishes his children. Jesus took the full measure of punishment for every Christian on the cross. The punishment we deserve for our sin has been poured out on Jesus. We are free. We are forgiven. We are sons and daughters.

If you overlook the extent of your own sin (for example: how self-centered your motives often are, and the corrupt desires of your heart), and if you downplay the extent of God's holiness (for example: his eternal perfection, beauty, and goodness) you can begin to feel like God's discipline is unfair, unnecessary, and unloving.

But if you honestly acknowledge how much sin you harbor in your heart, and if you recognize that God is preparing you to be with him, then you can rejoice in God's discipline, even as it exposes you to pain, hardship, and suffering. God loves his children, and he loves us enough to ready us for eternal joy with him.

When you find that you're despising God's discipline, remember that *the Lord disciplines those he loves, as a father does for the child he delights in.*

Let's pray together.

God,

I want to believe that I don't need any discipline. It's difficult for me to accept that I need to be molded, challenged, and changed. But when I honestly look into my heart, I do see selfish motives. I experience desires that are self-serving, and I have acted on those desires. I recognize that I am a sinner.

You understand all things perfectly. You know what tomorrow holds for me. You know what I truly need. Help me believe that. Help me accept that my understanding is very limited and that I don't see the world, or even my own life, as it really is.

Thank you for loving me even when I question you. Thank you for not disciplining me in anger. Give me a deeper faith so I can trust you, especially when you allow pain, hardship, and suffering into my life.

Amen.

Day 10

The Coming Judgment

Read Luke 11:29-32.

Jesus clearly taught that he was the only way to truly know God. He called himself *the* shepherd, *the* son of man, *the* vine, *the* lord of the Sabbath, *the* way, *the* truth, and *the* life. Jesus even went so far as to call himself greater than the temple – in fact, he claimed to be the *new* temple. God is not found in a building, but a person: Jesus Christ.

Many people who sat under the teaching of Jesus and witnessed

"When the crowds were increasing, he began to say, 'This generation is an evil generation. It seeks for a sign, but no sign will be given to it except the sign of Jonah. For as Jonah became a sign to the people of Nineveh, so will the Son of Man be to this generation. The queen of the South will rise up at the judgment with the men of this generation and condemn them, for she came from the ends of the earth to hear the wisdom of Solomon, and behold, something greater than Solomon is here. The men of Nineveh will rise up at the judgement with this generation and condemn it, for they repented at the preaching of Jonah, and behold, something greater than Jonah is here.'"

his miracles consistently asked for more 'signs and wonders.' But their curiosity was corrupt. Their hearts were hardened to God. They believed they were good enough people on their own – that

God was on their side, so to speak – and they trusted in their own wisdom. As a result, they were looking for every reason to *discount* Jesus' message. They didn't want to accept Jesus' teaching that they needed to *repent*.

So Jesus spoke some harsh words to them. *The people of Nineveh will condemn you at the Judgment because they repented when Jonah preached to them, and behold, someone greater than Jonah is preaching to you now.* Jesus called himself the greater Jonah.

Jesus also called himself the greater Solomon. *The Queen of Sheba will condemn you at the Judgment because she traveled very far to hear the wisdom of Solomon, and behold, someone far wiser than Solomon is speaking to you now.*

It's important to understand what Jesus meant when he said these things. He was essentially saying this: *'The people of Nineveh and the Queen of Sheba would have recognized that I am from God. They were ready to respond to God. But you are living in willful blindness and hardness of heart. That is why they will condemn you at the Judgment. They responded to Jonah and Solomon, but you have rejected me: the greater Jonah and the greater Solomon.'*

Jesus' point is rather clear. Those who reject Jesus will face God's judgment precisely for that reason – *because they have rejected him.* If Jesus was just an ordinary man, then this makes little sense. Why should someone face God's judgment for not listening to a mere human? There are many people we have decided to not listen to. We have given them a fair hearing, and we don't agree with them.

But if Jesus *is* the Son of God – now we're talking about something completely different. In this case, rejecting Jesus is the same as rejecting God. Not listening to Jesus is the same as ignoring God. Discounting the teachings of Jesus is the same as disregarding God. This is why Jesus said they would face judgment. By rejecting him, they were rejecting God.

Read Hebrews 10:28-29.

Perhaps you have heard someone say that the Old Testament is all about God's wrath, while the New Testament is all about God's grace. It *is* safe to say that God's wrath is more observable in the Old Testament and that his grace is more evident in the New Testament, but it is inaccurate to say that the New Testament is all about God's grace.

"Anyone who has set aside the law of Moses dies without mercy on the evidence of two or three witnesses. How much worse punishment, do you think, will be deserved by the one who has spurned the Son of God, and has profaned the blood of the covenant by which he was sanctified, and has outraged the Spirit of grace?"

On the contrary, God's wrath and judgment are *magnified* because of Jesus. Think about how Jesus treated the Old Testament law in the Sermon on the Mount. He said things like this: '*You have heard it said that you should not murder, but I say to you that if you hate someone, you have committed murder in your heart.*'

Jesus taught the same thing concerning adultery. '*You have heard it said that you should not commit adultery, but I say to you that if you lust after someone, you have committed adultery in your heart.*' Jesus did not weaken the law – he strengthened it. He magnified it. Jesus wanted every person to understand and accept this reality: You have sinned against God, you are a sinner, and *you need a savior.*

When we take the law seriously, we take Jesus seriously. That's why Jesus emphasized the law: to help us see that we desperately need his forgiveness. We need the power of his death and resurrection in our lives. We are guilty before God, and we need Jesus to save us from God's righteous judgment.

Jesus freely suffered and died on the cross to take away the power of sin. He died for people like you and me. The precious, perfect Son of God was crucified to take away the sin of the world. We must recognize him for who he is. He is worthy of our worship. He is the second Adam, the greater Moses, the final prophet, the Lamb of God, the King of Kings, the Prince of Peace, the Savior of the world.

If we reject Jesus, we reject God. And our judgment will be *more* severe under the New Testament. *How much worse punishment will be deserved by the one who has spurned the Son of God?*

Thinking on God's judgment is not enjoyable, but we need to take our cues from the Bible, not from our feelings or our culture. All of Scripture, and certainly the New Testament, talks about God's judgment quite frequently. We should keep it in our remembrance. It protects us from giving ourselves over to worthless pursuits and defiling desires.

Contrary to popular belief, a robust acceptance of God's judgment does not decrease the power of God's love. Instead, it deeply *increases* God's love by showing us how incredible it is that a God of such severe justice and radiant holiness delights in giving us grace and forgiveness. That will be our focus tomorrow.

Let's pray together.

God,

It's easy for me to forget that you deserve my worship, and that you have every right to demand it. When I think about my sin, I think about bad behaviors or destructive habits in my life. But I don't take the time to recognize that all my sin stems from failing to fully recognize who you are.

Protect me from my stubbornness. Don't allow me to harden my heart against you. Convict me when I engage in willful blindness – when I avoid facing you because I don't want to change or repent. Draw my heart to Jesus.

Thank you for sending Jesus to die for my sin and injustice. Thank you for your plan of salvation. Help me maintain a healthy remembrance of your coming judgment so I won't fall into useless idleness or callous indifference. Open my eyes to more fully see the radiance of your glory in Jesus.

Amen.

Day 11

Radical Forgiveness

Read Luke 6:27-28, 32-33.

"But I say to you who hear, Love your enemies, do good to those who hate you, bless those who curse you, pray for those who abuse you. If you love those who love you, what benefit is that to you? For even sinners love those who love them. And if you do good to those who do good to you, what benefit is that to you? For even sinners do the same."

All four of the gospel writers tell us about Peter's denial of Jesus. It's a bitter story of painful betrayal. Peter assured Jesus that he would never abandon him. He even said he was ready to follow Jesus into prison and death! Then, when Jesus was captured, three people asked Peter if he was Jesus' friend. Peter denied even knowing Jesus.

The Bible says that right after Peter denied Jesus the third time, Jesus looked at Peter. They gazed at one another. Peter looked at his friend, bruised and battered by his aggressive captors. When it really mattered – when it was time to pair actions with words – Peter betrayed Jesus, his dearest friend, the man who tirelessly invested in him without complaint or bitterness.

Have you ever been betrayed? When people hurt us in such a personal way, they usually become our enemies. We hold their betrayal against them. In some real way, they become dead to us. We do not wish for their good. Instead, we may be thrilled by the idea of them suffering.

How did Jesus handle his betrayal? *He forgave Peter*. Even more remarkable, he restored Peter. It wasn't a begrudging forgiveness. Jesus didn't say, '*Peter, I forgive you, but I'll never look at you the same way again*.' Jesus reinstated Peter as a disciple – and a friend.

Jesus tells us to love our enemies. What does that look like? He gives us three concrete examples. *Do good things for people who have done hateful things to you, speak kind words to people who have said awful things about you, and pray for the good of those who have hurt you*. Why should we feel compelled to live like this?

Jesus gives us some perspective. If we do good things only for people who have done good things for us, then we're loving people *according to their performance*. We are essentially saying, '*I will gladly do something good for you because you've done good to me. I love you based on your moral performance for me*.'

Everyone does that. That's not a powerful form of love, and perhaps not even real love at all. But when we do something good for someone who has been hateful to us – that is a completely different message. Now we are saying, '*I will serve you simply because you are a person made in God's image. You are valuable. I will love you in spite of your moral performance for me*.'

It's easy to forget that God *always* loves us in this costly way. He loves us in spite of our moral performance. He doesn't do good to us after we've proved ourselves. On the contrary, he is ready and willing to forgive us and restore us, even if our whole life has been one episode after another of disappointing moral failure.

God's forgiveness is radical because he really does love his enemies. If he didn't, then none of us would be here. He would have already judged us for our sin and sent us to hell. God blesses people who curse him. He gives good things to people who hate him. He loves people who despise him. God forgives and restores those who betray him.

Read Matthew 6:14-15.

> "For if you forgive others their trespasses, your heavenly Father will also forgive you, but if you do not forgive others their trespasses, neither will your Father forgive your trespasses."

The way we treat others is directly connected to what we think about God. For instance, God fervently values truth. He *is* truth. There is no deception in him. The ninth commandment tells us we should not lie about another person, or lie to another person. Why? Because God values truth. He upholds honesty. He treasures integrity.

So when we lie, we are not only sinning against a person: we are sinning against God. Our heart attitude says, '*God, I don't care that you value truth. Your character means little to me. I have decided to lie, and what you think doesn't matter.*' When we treat someone poorly by lying to them or about them, we are revealing what we think about God in that moment.

This helps to explain Jesus' teaching on forgiveness. *If you do not forgive others, neither will God forgive you.* Imagine a Christian who exults in her forgiveness. She talks about how much she values God's love and his radical forgiveness. Yet, at the same time, she refuses to forgive people who have done hateful things to her.

By refusing to forgive others, she reveals how she *really* feels about God. She doesn't recognize how costly it was for God to forgive her – that he sacrificed his only son to take away her sin. She doesn't really value that God loves her in spite of *her* moral performance. She doesn't acknowledge the depth of her own sin and realize that she doesn't deserve forgiveness from God.

When we withhold forgiveness from others, we show that we neither appreciate nor value God's forgiveness in our own lives. If we did, we would forgive others. If we recognized that God loved us in such a costly way by forgiving us, in spite of our many failures to love him, then we wouldn't be hard-hearted towards others.

Our hearts would say, *'God forgave me, at the cost of Jesus' life, even though I didn't deserve it. He loved me in spite of my performance. So how can I withhold forgiveness from you if God didn't withhold it from me?'*

Forgiveness is not easy. We cannot truly practice forgiveness unless we are reminding ourselves regularly of God's radical forgiveness for us through Christ. Through Jesus and Jesus alone we can be forgiven. Go to Jesus in faith. He will not withhold forgiveness from you.

Let's pray together.

God,

It's hard for me to accept that I should do good to people who have been hateful to me. When someone wrongs me, I don't want to pray for their good. I want them to be punished. When someone commits an injustice against me, I feel like they need to suffer in some way for their failure to treat me well.

But I have wronged you by sinning against you more times than I can count, and you still want what's best for me. I have wounded your heart many times, and you don't write me off. I have committed injustices against you and others, and you were never eager to make me suffer. You were eager to forgive me and restore me.

Thank you for your radical forgiveness. Help me to more fully see and accept the depth of my own sin, and to recognize that your forgiveness is not cheap. Jesus died to forgive me. Am I withholding forgiveness from someone? Expose my hard-heartedness. Teach me to love people the way you do.

Amen.

Day 12

All Authority

Read Matthew 28:18-20.

"And Jesus came and said to them, 'All authority in heaven and on earth has been given to me. Go therefore and make disciples of all nations, baptizing them in the name of the Father and of the Son and of the Holy Spirit, teaching them to observe all that I have commanded you. And behold, I am with you always, to the end of the age.'"

After his resurrection from the dead, Jesus prepared his disciples for his departure. He was going to ascend into heaven to once again be in the immediate presence of his Father. Jesus assured his disciples that he would always be with them, and that he was – and always would be – in charge of all things. *All authority in heaven and on earth has been given to me.*

Jesus also instructed his disciples to dedicate themselves to one primary task: help people become functional Christians who walk with God in their everyday lives by teaching them to obey the things I have commanded. That's what it practically looks like to make disciples.

According to Jesus, he has all authority over everything – spiritual and physical. And he has given us commands that he intends for us to obey. If we put this together in one simple sentence, we could say this: *Jesus has the authority to tell us how we ought to live.*

The word 'ought' is very appropriate here. Jesus doesn't just *want* you to obey him. He doesn't merely *hope* you will listen to him. He is not offering helpful advice he would *like* you to consider. It's much more concrete than that. Jesus has all authority, and he has given us commands – things we ought to do.

Read 1 Corinthians 6:19-20.

The Corinthian church in Paul's day struggled with sexual ethics. They mistakenly believed that how they used their bodies had no effect upon their spiritual condition. Paul wanted them to understand that God had authority over how they practiced their sexuality. *Do you not know that the Holy Spirit lives in you? You are not your own because God bought you at the price of Jesus' blood. So glorify God with your body.*

> "Or do you not know that your body is a temple of the Holy Spirit within you, whom you have from God? You are not your own, for you were bought with a price. So glorify God in your body."

In our culture, it's fairly easy to help most people understand that we should be kind to others, and be generous with those in need, and refrain from judging people based on their ethnicity. All these behaviors involve us acting morally toward someone else: respecting them, being charitable to them, and treating them with kindness and respect.

It's much more difficult to help people understand that God lays claim to their *personal life*. God has the authority to judge our personal desires. He calls some of them good and commands us to grow in them, and he calls others wicked and commands us to flee from them. He has the authority to tell us what we ought to do with our time, our talents, and our money. God claims the authority to speak into the most personal parts of our lives.

God is not only concerned with how we treat others. He certainly cares about how we relate to other people, but he also cares about how we personally relate to *him*. God has every right to say to us, *'You must treat others as you want to be treated,'* and *'You must repent of and flee from every personal desire that dishonors me.'*

Read Luke 12:4-5.

> "I tell you, my friends, do not fear those who kill the body, and after that have nothing more that they can do. But I will warn you whom to fear: fear him who, after he has killed, has authority to cast into hell. Yes, I tell you, fear him!"

It's important for us to remember that God's authority is tethered to his grace and forgiveness. When Jesus healed a paralytic man in Mark's gospel, he also forgave the man's sins. The religious leaders said to themselves, *'How can Jesus have the authority to forgive sins?'* Because Jesus has all authority, he *can* forgive sins. He can offer grace to sinners. He can redeem the broken.

We must hold Jesus' grace *and* authority in the same hand. We can only receive grace from Jesus because he has the authority to give it. And because Jesus has the authority to give us grace, he *also* has the authority to tell us how we ought to live. We can't separate one from the other. If Jesus has no real authority, then he cannot forgive our sins. But if he does have real authority, then he can forgive our sins *and* command us to live according to his wisdom.

We cannot claim to have God's forgiveness, and at the same time, assert that Jesus has no authority over how we use our bodies, minds, and hearts. Sometimes we fall into dangerous indifference towards God. We imagine that his love gives us the license to live in whatever way we see fit.

When we stumble into such foolishness, God's authority warns us and protects us from coming under his judgment. *Don't fear mere people who can only kill your body. Fear God who has the authority to kill your body and cast you into hell.* God's authority comforts us when we feel as though the world is out of control, and his authority warns us when we falsely imagine that Jesus has no say over how we live.

At the final Judgment, God's authority will be both celebrated and despised. Every authentic Christian will celebrate God's authority – his power to redeem all creation and raise us to new life in a restored world where sin, suffering, and death have no dominion. But all who reject Jesus' authority in this life will despise God's authority at the Judgment. By his authority, God will strip every good thing from them for all eternity.

This is hard for us to accept, but we cannot act as though Jesus is silent on the matter. His words are abundantly clear: *Whoever seeks to preserve his life will lose it, but whoever loses his life will keep it.* Lose your life to Jesus. Freely surrender all authority to him. Hold nothing back. You won't regret it.

Let's pray together.

God,

I have a tendency to reduce you to a sage or a life coach – someone who gives me helpful advice and cheers me on. I am comfortable with that image of you because it doesn't challenge my own ideas of how I want to live and who I want to be. But you're not just a teacher, and you're certainly more than a cheerleader. You have all authority over everything, including me.

I need your authority in my life to comfort me and to warn me. Remind me often of your promise that you will never leave any person who trusts you. Remind me that you are in control of all things. At the same time, open my eyes to more fully see the reality that you have authority over what I do with my body, my mind, and my heart; my time, my talents, and my treasure.

Thank you for using your authority to forgive my sin. Thank you for being a God who doesn't abuse authority. Help me to accept that I am not my own, that I was created by you and that you bought me at the incredible cost of Jesus' blood. Teach me to submit to your authority the way Jesus submitted his entire life to you.

Amen.

Day 13

Righteous Anger

Read Deuteronomy 9:6-8.

"Know, therefore, that the Lord your God is not giving you this good land to possess because of your righteousness, for you are a stubborn people. Remember and do not forget how you provoked the Lord your God to wrath in the wilderness. From the day you came out of the land of Egypt until you came to this place, you have been rebellious against the Lord. Even at Horeb you provoked the Lord to wrath, and the Lord was so angry with you that he was ready to destroy you."

There are many who find it difficult to accept that God is capable of anger. They envision a loving God, and in their view, a loving God is inconsistent with anger. Sometimes a person feels this way because they've only ever witnessed sinful anger – a rash, hateful, immature anger. They mistakenly assume that God's anger is similar.

The reality is that God's anger is always *righteous*. He is angered by sin, injustice, and pride, among other things, because they misrepresent God and destroy what he has made. They ruin what is good and cause great damage.

After God miraculously freed the Israelites from Egypt, he provided them food and water. He guided their steps with a pillar of cloud by day and a pillar of fire by night. He was taking them to a promised land, a place they could call their own and raise their families in peace. But all along the way, the people rebelled against God.

They constantly complained. They were always discontent with what God provided. They were stubborn, full of themselves, and insistent on doing things their way. Even though God was continually pouring out his goodness to them and blessing them – providing them with food and water they couldn't provide for themselves – they took every opportunity to assert their arrogant independence.

At one point, Moses ascended a mountain called Sinai (also called Horeb) to meet with God. He was gone for only 40 days. While Moses was away, the people of Israel constructed a golden calf and began to worship it. They acted disgracefully and made sacrifices to the work of their hands. *They worshiped what they had made.* After all that God had provided, they so quickly abandoned him to make a god that they could control.

God was very angry with the people for their sin. It's not that God's feelings were hurt, as if he needs people to like him in order to feel worthy. It wasn't a petty anger. God was angry because the Israelites were so callous and haughty and defiant. God had graciously chosen them as his people so they could show the world what it looks like to know the one, true God. Instead of setting a worthy example, they acted disgracefully.

They were defiant, hard-hearted, set on doing things their way, full of greed, hungry for control, unteachable, stubborn, and arrogant. God's presence was with them, and he saw to all their needs. He was working to raise up a people who could show the world what it looks like to love deeply, act righteously, and live humbly with wisdom.

God was rightful in his anger because the people were grievously misrepresenting the God who redeemed them, and they were destroying themselves because of their great arrogance.

God's righteous anger is similar to his *jealousy*. God is called a 'jealous God,' or is said to have jealousy for his people about ten times in the Bible. Once again, sometimes a person has trouble reconciling this characteristic with a loving God because they think of sinful examples of jealousy. They imagine God as an immature boy in middle school who can't stand it when Sally notices other boys.

God's jealousy doesn't make sense unless we consider all the ways he describes himself. God, for example, calls himself a Father: and so he loves us simply because we are his children and disciplines us as a good father would. God also calls himself a Creator: so he reminds us that we are his creatures. In the same way, God calls himself a *husband*: he is jealous for our affection just as a husband longs for faithful love from his wife.

Read Hosea 2:16-20.

"And in that day, declares the Lord, you will call me 'My Husband,' and no longer will you call me 'My Baal.' For I will remove the names of the Baals from her mouth, and they shall be remembered by name no more. And I will make for them a covenant on that day with the beasts of the field, the birds of the heavens, and the creeping things of the ground. And I will abolish the bow, the sword, and war from the land, and I will make you lie down in safety. And I will betroth you to me forever. I will betroth you to me in righteousness and in justice, in steadfast love and in mercy."

In this Old Testament prophecy God is foreshadowing the beauty of heaven, and he says that his people will call him *"My Husband."* It's a beautiful image of God's love for his people. *He lies us down in safety. He is faithful to us forever. He is ever righteous for us and always full of justice. We shall know the Lord with complete intimacy, as a husband and wife know one another.*

This explains why God is jealous for us: *he loves us.* He sent Jesus to die for us and raised him from the dead. God has made a way for us to know him. He is wooing us, desiring us, calling us to lay down our arrogance and submit to him. He is jealous for us as a husband jealously desires that his wife's greatest affections would be for him and not another man. That's not petty. That's beautiful, intimate love.

God still has righteous anger today, and there is only one way to avoid his wrath – by turning in faith to Jesus and trusting him to forgive your sin. Without the forgiveness of Christ, you must go before God at the Judgment and explain why you deserve to know a God of such perfection in light of all your sin. It will not go well. God will damn you, and he will be righteous in his judgment.

God is love, and God is justice. In his love and immense grace, he has made a way for us to become right with him through faith in Jesus. If, in our arrogance, we reject his offer of forgiveness in Jesus, then we cannot fault him. The problem is *never* that God fails to love. The problem is *always* that we are very slow to lay down our stubborn pride.

Let's pray together.

———————————— ◆ ————————————

God,

When it comes to specific sins, I can accept the idea of your righteous anger. I can easily accept that a man who bombs a school full of children deserves your anger. It's much more difficult for me to accept that your righteous anger could be in my life, against my sin, because it just doesn't seem that bad compared to major atrocities.

But you are a God of perfect justice. All sin is rebellion against you, and though I may not have ever committed a great atrocity, I have acted pridefully. The same pride that can drive a person to kill is in my heart. I can be stubborn, set in my own ways, hard-hearted to others, and unteachable. My sin deserves your righteous anger.

Thank you for being a jealous God – a God who loves his people like a faithful husband loves his wife. Draw my heart to yours. Protect me from lesser loves, from idols of wealth and approval and sinful pleasure. Woo my heart, speak to me. Teach me how to lay down my pride. Thank you for Jesus and his great sacrifice, which came at such a high cost to you, and is freely given to me.

Amen.

Day 14

Boundless Compassion

Read Matthew 23:37.

"O Jerusalem, Jerusalem, the city that kills the prophets and stones those who are sent to it! How often would I have gathered your children together as a hen gathers her brood under her wings, and you would not!"

Jesus was always facing major opposition and discouragement. The religious leaders, who should have been the *most* ready to recognize Jesus as God, were the *least* willing. They lived in a web of deceitful self-righteousness and couldn't understand why God would desire to know sinners. They, of course, were blind to their own sin, and so they were hostile toward Jesus.

The political elites were threatened by Jesus because his words were powerful and influential. He consistently stirred up conflict with politicians who cared very little for serving people but cared very much about appeasing them. Many leaders feared the impact of Jesus' ministry because it provoked so much social unrest, and they didn't want Rome to revoke their authority.

The common people were constantly pulling Jesus in multiple directions, and their motives for seeking him out were often shoddy.

They didn't want to know God. They just wanted a healing, or a meal, or a captivating speech. They didn't so much want to know Jesus; they just wanted what he could provide. So when Jesus told them to repent and live for more than worldly comfort and pleasure, they were put off.

It's not difficult to see why so many called out for Jesus' crucifixion. The religious leaders were offended by him. The political elites were jealous of him. The common people grew weary of him. They didn't want to deny themselves and obey God, and they were tired of feeling convicted by their sin in Jesus' presence. So they all cried out in unison, "*Crucify him! Crucify him!*"

Before Jesus carried his cross, he already knew what was coming. He knew why the Father had sent him, and he was ready to fulfill the plan of redemption: to die for the sin of the world. It's hard to believe that in light of all Jesus knew, he *still* felt great compassion for the people who were stubbornly rejecting him.

You stubborn people who silence those who speak truth and suppress what you know is right. How eagerly I want to know you! How strongly I desire to redeem you! I have poured out everything to show you who I am, and I'll even die a criminal's death for your sin, and yet, you still will not come to me. I would joyfully take you, but you won't have me!

The compassion of Jesus is *remarkable*. He was so in-tune with the needs of everyone around him. He slowed down to help, heal, and teach at his own cost, on his own time. He had no home. He had no comfort. His family was embarrassed by him. His society wanted him only for what he could give, but didn't care for him as a person.

Yet, he compassionately gave, and gave, and gave. He even freely gave his life to save us, and as he was dying on the cross, he cried out for his Father to *forgive* those who were murdering him. That is boundless compassion.

Read John 11:32-35.

"Now when Mary came to where Jesus was and saw him, she fell at his feet, saying to him, 'Lord, if you had been here, my brother would not have died.' When Jesus saw her weeping, and the Jews who had come with her also weeping, he was deeply moved in his spirit and greatly troubled. And he said, 'Where have you laid him?' They said to him, 'Lord, come and see.' Jesus wept."

One of the more well-known stories in the New Testament is Jesus raising Lazarus from the dead. If you rush through the story, you can't really capture the depth of Jesus' compassion. Though he knew he was about to raise his friend from the dead, he saw the pain of those around him and was both deeply moved and greatly troubled.

He was deeply moved because *he felt what they felt.* Jesus is the most empathetic person who ever lived, and still today, he understands your pain and sorrow *better* than you do. Jesus didn't rush around. He didn't try to explain away their tears. He slowed down, joined his friends, and wept along with them. Jesus is present in our pain more than we know, and *no one* understands pain and sorrow more fully than Jesus.

He was also greatly troubled because he saw the horrible brokenness of this world. Death, though natural, is one of the most unnatural things in human experience. It's horrible. The curse of sin in this world has marred so much, and Jesus was troubled by it. He wasn't troubled because he didn't understand how to fix it – he was troubled because it was so awful to see God's good creation tarnished by sin and death.

Read Hebrews 2:14.

The beauty of the Gospel is that all of God's characteristics are most profoundly seen in the *death and resurrection of Jesus.* God's love is nowhere more evident than in Jesus' sacrificial death. God's justice is nowhere more apparent than in Jesus' atonement on the cross. God's forgiveness is nowhere more moving than in Jesus' willingness to die for us.

> "Since therefore the children share in flesh and blood, he himself likewise partook of the same things, that through death he might destroy the one who has the power of death, that is, the devil."

In the same way, God's power is nowhere more magnified than in the resurrection of Jesus. God's grace is nowhere more thrilling than in the Savior who conquered death so we could escape it. God's faithfulness is nowhere more beautiful than in the risen Christ who perfectly fulfilled all the promises of God.

We are creatures of flesh and blood. *Jesus partook of the same things.* He became like us *and died* so he could destroy the devil and defeat death itself. Just like every other characteristic of God, his compassion is nowhere more remarkable than in Jesus' death and resurrection. God made a way for us to live forever with him, and he did it at *his own cost.* His compassion is truly boundless. Submit to the love of Jesus and find real peace.

Let's pray together.

God,

The depth of your compassion is both comforting and convicting. I am comforted by your compassion because I'm reminded that you know me. You understand my hardship and suffering better than I do. And rather than just telling me to dry my tears and get over it, you walk with me through the pain and weep with me. Thank you for your compassion.

At the same time, I am convicted by your compassion because my attention is so often focused on me. I don't feel for people the way you do. I don't slow down to serve and love people at my own expense often enough. I need your help to do that. Fill my heart with your powerful, sacrificial compassion.

Thank you for feeling great compassion for your enemies: I was at one time your enemy. I didn't know you, I was blindly living in my sin, and I was hostile to your work in my life. Thank you for pursuing me. Teach me how to have that kind of compassion for people in my life.

Amen.

Day 15

God on Mission

Read 1 Peter 2:9.

We cannot understand the purpose of the church apart from this reality: *God is on mission.* God didn't form the church and then give the church freedom to decide its purpose. Instead, God planned a mission and

"But you are a chosen race, a royal priesthood, a holy nation, a people for his own possession, that you may proclaim the excellencies of him who called you out of darkness into his marvelous light."

then raised up the church as his means for completing it. God is *personally* on this mission, and he has invited the church to join him.

What's the mission? God is redeeming the world. *How is he redeeming it?* Through his Son, Jesus Christ. God is at work, reversing sin and death. This mission was planned before all time, but it officially began with the resurrection of Jesus. The Bible calls Jesus the firstborn from the dead. Jesus marks the beginning of this great reversal: Jesus died, and God reversed it. He wasn't just restored to his previous body. He was given a resurrection body, *eternally resistant* to sin and death.

That's what eternity is going to be: *a huge reversal*. All the terrible effects of sin will be removed. All wrongs will be made right. All hearts will be exposed. The motives for every action will be judged. The dead from every age of mankind will be raised to stand judgment before the God of the universe, and justice will prevail. There will be no mistrials.

At that time, all sin will be punished in one of two ways. Every person who trusted in the righteousness of Jesus will be acquitted for their sin because their punishment was borne by Jesus on the cross. They faced their sin, accepted their guilt, repented for their wickedness, and trusted Jesus and his righteousness.

On the other hand, everyone who justified their sinful deeds and refused to submit to Christ will have to bear their *own* punishment. All of us have wounded God's heart and have hurt others with our sin – every person has caused damage with their pride, gossip, lies, hateful anger, envy, adultery, cruelty, and so on. No one is exempt from this. If our sin is not covered by the death of Christ, we must bear our own punishment for the wounds we've caused.

This explains why the mission of God is so *cosmically* important. Every person you know is an eternal being. They will live *forever*, either with God in heaven, or in the anguish of hell. This is why God is always at work, growing his church. He is constantly building a people who will join him on mission. God has called us to him so we can introduce the world to the one, true God.

You have been chosen, you are a royal son or daughter of God, you have been made holy by Jesus' sacrifice, you are a prized possession of God. Why? Why has God chosen you, and adopted you as his child, and made you holy through the work of Christ? *So that you can joyfully and boldly tell others how God pulled you out of your darkness and brought you into the marvelous light of his presence.*

It's rather astounding to think about what Peter is saying. God has worked powerfully in your life and has brought you to himself *for the express purpose* of you proclaiming God's goodness to the world, telling others how he overcame your darkness and brought you into the light. In other words, God redeemed you so that you could join him in redeeming the world.

[64]

Read 1 Corinthians 7:17.

Sometimes when we imagine what it would look like to live on mission with God, we imagine a life that is utterly different from our own. We imagine

> "Only let each person lead the life that the Lord has assigned to him, and to which God has called him. This is my rule in all the churches."

moving to a foreign country or starting a benevolent non-profit. These are certainly ways of living on mission, but we don't have to make it that complicated.

God has put people in your life. You are surrounded by people who you regularly interact with. You can live on mission in those relationships right now, and *you should*. By the way you live, you proclaim what you believe and what you value. By the words you speak, you can introduce others to the grace & truth of Jesus. To live on mission you need only two things: *a real faith in Jesus and a real love for people*.

If you have those two things, mission will happen. You will care too much about the people in your life to *not* talk about how God's grace has changed you. You will experience a freedom in Christ that will compel you to share the hope of the Gospel. You will pray for them when they come to your mind, and you will have a desire to see them come into a saving relationship with Jesus.

God has assigned you a particular place in life. *Where*? Right where you are! In time, he may lead you elsewhere, but for now, this is where you are. You can be on mission with him *now*.

Recognizing that God is on mission is the engine of Christian love. We are reminded that we know God only because we heard and obeyed the Gospel at some point. We were once in darkness. Our mission is to show others how God overcame our darkness with the power of Jesus' love, authority, and forgiveness. We speak boldly, and we speak humbly – motivated by a love for God and a love for others.

Let's pray together.

God,

It's exciting to think about you on mission. Since the fall of mankind, you have been at work, bringing to pass your plan of redemption. You made a promise to Abraham that through him the world would be blessed, and through his lineage came your Son, Jesus. Your plan of redemption is currently in progress, and you've invited me to join you!

Remind me that I was once in darkness and that someone took the time to help me understand the Gospel. Take away all my self-righteousness against other people and replace it with a genuine love. Help me feel a godly love for those who don't yet know you, so I will yearn to see them brought into the beautiful light of your presence.

Awaken me to the missional opportunities that are in my life right now. Work in my heart so my love for you and my love for others will grow. Thank you for being a God on mission – if you weren't, I wouldn't know you. Thank you for pursuing me. Thank you for putting people in my life who showed me how you overcame their darkness. Equip me to share my story with humility and boldness.

Amen.

Epilogue

The last two sentences of John's gospel provide some perspective on how much there is to say about who God is:

"Now there are also many other things that Jesus did. Were every one of them to be written, I suppose that the world itself could not contain the books that would be written."

This book falls utterly short of capturing who God is. It's just one humble resource. It has aimed at putting some characteristics of God on display that are sometimes overlooked in our cultural context.

When it comes to knowing God, it's great to search for books, articles, blogs, and sermons that help to explain what the Bible says. But that's all those resources can do: they are just explaining what's in the Bible. You cannot replace the immeasurable value of reading the Bible, meditating on it, and prayerfully meeting God there.

I'll give C. S. Lewis the final word:

"It is quite right to go away from [the Bible] for a moment in order to make some special point clear. But you must always go back. Naturally God knows how to describe Himself much better than we know how to describe Him." – *Mere Christianity*, book four, "Good Infection."

www.ingramcontent.com/pod-product-compliance
Lightning Source LLC
Chambersburg PA
CBHW021220020426
42331CB00003B/400